Salutations of Soulitude

PATRICIA YOUNGS

Trafford
PUBLISHING® www.trafford.com
North America & international
toll-free: 1 888 232 4444 (USA & Canada)
fax: 812 355 4082

Poetry
baptizes
language
with its
clear flow of
words
to
mind
the senses anew

Dedication

This book is dedicated to the virtual online
world of blogs and profiles.

Contents

First Words 1
   Cemetery Bunny.. 1
   Opilies.. 4
   Digging Dirt... 5
   Sick... 6
   Subconscious Seeds... 7
   Half Empty Glass Half Full, acrostic 8
   Flip Side... 10
   No Tomorrow 11
   Guillotine Ghost... 12
   Pumpkin Head 13

Sleeping In Overdrive... 14
   Will Power.. 14
   Slices of Bread without Butter 17
   Note Left Behind.. 18
   Mountain Truth Hurts 19
   Spin Cycle.. 20
   U - 10^9 21
   Ode to Two Chairs 22
   Tilling the Brain Waves 23
   The State of Sleeping.. 24
   Family Jewels 25
   The Milk Man's Daughter.. 26
   Marble Eyes See Nothing.. 27
   Love Story... 28

Mosaic Stars...29
Fat Girl..30
Happy Mother's Day..31
Staining the Sheets..32
Clips of You..33
Who's He Fooling? 34
Hat on a Hot Head..35
Population Overgrowth 37
Corner Store Dog 38
Impromptu Rehearsal 39
Flip and Flop 40
Dear Grandpa (I'll Never Tell)......................................41
Scratch Ticket..42
Wasted Wax Offerings...43
Freedom Cell 44
Lava Monster..45
Dinner Bell..46
One Serving Recommended Daily..................................48
Haiku 49
Tanka 50
Recipe for Snowflake Cake 51
Unrequited Love...52
Truth 53

Sovereign Souvenirs...54
Instructions for My Son's Art Project 54
Cup of Joe..55
Untitled 1 56
Extra! Extra! Pope Sells Out...57
Brown Colored Crayons...58
Deaf and Blind 60
Where Charlie Was Born..61
Poised Sugar For Sale..62
Williamesque Skipping Down Memory Lane
With That Story From Oh, Didn't Know........................63
Polar Bear with a Heart-Shaped Brain 65

Devil S Muse 66
Getting to the World Race on Time 67
Lady Duck and Mister Goose 69
Little Dog on a Full Moon.. 70
All Caterpillars are Free 71
Girls Who Talk to Too Much 72
Mother at Midnight.. 73
Of a Bird I Never Met 74
Perennial Sketches of Me, pantoum 75
Flower Shop, dialogue.. 76
My Cousin It 77
Little Stream of Consciousness from a Greatly
Delusional Firecracker 78
Roses in an Open Window 79
Post Landing Questionnaire 80
For April, acrostic 81
Missionary Rapist Frac King... 82
Apple Tree in December 83
Autumn Leaves Glitter Notes 84
Numbing Circus... 85
Dance to an Invisible Backdrop 86
Bats Eat Bugs... 87
Can You Hear Me Now.. 88
Carnal Earthlings Are Hungry - Pantoum 89
Children of the Fire 90
For Winter Solstice 2013 - Sestina 91
Lighthouse Tide.. 93
Lion's Lace 94
On Peace, Sestina 95
Funny Dollar..97
Morning Stroll..98
Mystic Ocean Land 99
New Mexico Sunset – Greetings from the
Swimming Pool 100
Pencil... 101
Pot of Gold Rain Bubbles 102

Star Man.. 103
Sunrise Fire Death 104
China Bull – Flash Fiction.......................... 105
For Matt R. Rocks...................................... 107
The Starfish That Got Away.......................... 108
R.E. Kooh 109
Unit-Tee's Angel.. 110
On Wings - Prose 111
Wet flower 112
Wild Cat at the Card Table........................... 113
Fisherman's Prick; Scorpio in Pisces............. 114
Black Coffee Guts..115
She Cried.. 116
Not Always With Love 117
Stuck In the House....................................... 118
Want To See My O-0 Boa Constrictor? 119
Frankenstein's Sacrifice 120
Lou's House on the Right 121
Train to Buddha Fest.................................... 122
The End.. 123

First Words

Cemetery Bunny

Josephine was a scruffy old brown bunny sitting quietly in a corner of the petting zoo content to be left alone. She had always wanted to escape the hectic zoo. It was full of children wanting to pet and feed her dried green pellets which at first she hated, but grew to eat them because it meant the children would eventually go away.

Josephine never did understand why Rose, a young girl who fed her fresh greens and hay sprinkled with sweet petals in her bowl and let her roam the house, left her there one day. Joesphine appreciated two zoo caretakers, Katherine and Janice. They fed her every morning with fresh lettuce and bits of carrot and gave everyone a warm cheerful hello. It was rest of the day Josephine could live without.

When Janice started cleaning up the garbage left behind by visitors that day, she noticed Josephine in the corner. She softly asked her to move, but the bunny would not budge. Janice let her be.

Twilight was approaching when Josephine fell into a deep sleep. Her heartbeat slowed to an undetectable rate. She began to dream she was curiously sniffing the gate, when it swung wide-open inviting her out to freedom. She thought, "This is my big moment." As she hopped out the gate, she felt excited and scared at the same time, hoping to find the most delicious food in the world: flowers. She especially loved their soft velvety petals.

She found herself surrounded by lots of white bunnies in a dark forest. "Hi," they squealed.

Josephine asked them, "Where are the flowers?"

"Someday soon we'll show you where to find the best flowers in the world, but first let's dance and play!" the bunnies playfully answered in unison. Josephine happily danced with them, but soon they faded away.

She came to the edge of another thick forest and saw that it transcended upwards. She slowly climbed up, finally making her way to the very top, where she looked down to see a beautiful huge lawn dotted with flowers off in the distance. Her ears perked up and her eyes grew bright and round. She knew the smell delicious flowers, the best in the world so close to the sky. Her nose twitched and sniffed her way right to them.

On her way she met the same white bunnies she had seen earlier in her dream. They lived right next to the carefully manicured lawns full of roses, gladiolas, and carnations with cut stems placed neatly in heavy vases flanking tombstone markers. Dandelions grew in patches of sweet clover in the shade. Her new bunny friends squealed with delight, "You really found us this time!"

Josephine's pain magically subsided. She felt she was no longer the aged brown bunny but instead young and happy again. Her new friends told her about the solemn people dressed in black who came every day and carefully placed fresh-cut flowers out on the lawn. They came in groups or just one person. The bunnies thought it was the funniest game to find the fresh flowers. Every day was perfect, and the dream never ended.

The next morning, Katherine came around to open the gate. The animals were aware a new day was upon them. "Hi, Josephine", called Katherine, as she noticed the old brown bunny still in the same corner from the day before. Katherine became worried and called over her co-worker Janice. The two of them leaned over Josephine.

"Josephine, wake up," they said in hopeful whispers.

Josephine was not waking up. Katherine became quite upset her voice quivering with sadness until she started sobbing uncontrollably, "Josephine is gone. She died."

"Don't worry," Janice said, "Josephine is surrounded by hundreds of flowers. She's one of those bunnies you hear about at the cemetery. We can go there tonight and place some flowers just for her, OK?"

That evening, the two women slipped through the closed cemetery gate. Out of the corner of her eye, Katherine caught a glimpse of a small brown bunny hopping high, joy abounding with a group of white bunnies. She looked again and saw nothing. They put down a dozen carnations mixed with dandelions and hay for Josephine and left silently. Katherine said to Janice, "I feel better now. I think I saw Josephine and she looked very happy."

Opilies

Wagging tail and happy smile,
innocent eyes all the while
the world spins its evil grin.
Oblivious. My heart you win.

Digging Dirt

How you like to dig
up my flower gems.
Bring them here to me
I must cut their stems.
These roses of mine
are treated like weeds.
If I had the time
I would plant large trees.
You could dig the holes
and do as you please.

Sick

I am sick of people
who can't think for themselves
Sick of being in a rut.
Sick of avoidance.
When life appears pointless,
what does it matter if
there is nothing to say.
I am sick of it all.
Just sit, don't ask, don't tell.
of invisibility,
of silence, of stillness,
I am sick of living like this.
Pick up your feet.
Walk where people can see you
hear you, love you, hate you.
Tell me I am not sick.

Subconscious Seeds

I'd like to take you to my garden
See the blue, green, purple and red?
Open the gate. It's dark in there. Dark like the words of silence
running
through my head, like how
cemeteries live eternal
offering buried hearts to
the living colors, forever changing,
mixing into something new.

HALF EMPTY GLASS HALF FULL, acrostic

Kneeling as I pray for strength to control the
Anger and pain in my heart while I listen to
Instructions on how I must simply wait as my
Sister keeps crying uncontrollably at the bedside,
Enduring like I am the uncertainty of our mother's
Right to die or live, I am not sure of anything.

Hell is here, tightening my heart today.
Oh God, please take her from this place of
Suffering. But no, the surgeon tells me her
Plight may end in happiness and she may
Indeed live again. How can this be when
Twenty IV bags are hanging, her lungs
And kidneys are not working and all
Life has disappeared from her body?

Can this be the reality of the 21st century.
All knowledge put in machines that
Replace human function for months, weeks,
Days on end. Their sounds scare me. It's too much.
I had no idea it would come to this
Obscene huffing and clicking of a
Ventilator, nitrous oxide,
And a continuous veno-venous hemofiltration machine
Synchronized to computers that control medications.
Could it really be true all this can make Frankenstein come alive?
Unknowing, unsure, I stay strong for my mother at her bedside and
Leave it to God and modern medicine to say yeah or nay,
Although deep down I wish for a peaceful ending, no heroics, no
Rush to intubate or resuscitate. But this is not for me. It is for my
mother.

In one month, three weeks, and four days, her heart begins to pull through.
Now I begin to see the light at the end of this long, long dark tunnel.
Tell me, doctor, is she really going to make it. His crystal ball says yes.
Elated, I kneel and pray thanking God while angels
Nod their heads yes, my mother is coming back to us.
Sun shined in hell the day my mother slowly wrote, "WATER please".
Intubated and disoriented, she wanted to live. I smiled in
Victory. I felt I went to the moon. I floated out of the hospital.
Each step was light and airy.
Come in, said the nurse after I waited for the buzzer to let me in.
All is looking well for your mother, but she'll need long-term
Rehabilitation. I am willing to wait another year for
Each day with my mother is a second chance at life.

© 6/23/05 ~ My mother passed away 10/28/05

Flip Side

I killed like a gangsta.
Uprooted a life.
Killed the evidence.
I wanted freedom.
I had no guilt.
They say I was wrong.
What's wrong are the
righteous who carry
a torch in the name
of Jesus and the
book he left behind.
I leave behind nothing.
No footprint
that bares liking
to me or the man
who planted the seed.
There is just me
walking this earth
watching the sun shine
on the blood shed in the
name of war and
greed and power
and wealth.

Thank you Science,
for sparing the world
another child
it does not need
witnessing the
struggle of those
like me who
live on the other
side of the coin.

My side -
the side not called to win the toss.

No Tomorrow

It only takes a second to leave
Mother Earth's ageless love and sin.
Sometimes it takes years to believe.
It's hard to know where to begin.

Is it with the speeding driver or
the red brake lights
red, red like the red dripping out of my
little dog's mouth, his body limp
in my arms as he sighed his last breath
like my mother did when that second came and she left me.

I don't know why, I only know I feel better when I cry.

Guillotine Ghost

There's a devil in my attic.
I put him there.
I used to dance and play with him.
He will not leave.

He sits next to an old record player
and a dingy notebook full of words.
No more waste of innocent lust.
There is no door to shut.

He stands there,
hand out inviting me to do it again.
Look away, little sunshine, look away.
Cracks split open, he falls through the floor.

Pumpkin Head

Darkness reaches his pointy fingernail to tap on the lid,
wants to wake up the passion that tears his soul from guts
wrenched in between fooled hearts of madness,
pinches the knots gnarled inside the spines of the spine
entered in right up through the hole at the bottom.
The brittle tip aged with multitudes of lines making
giant redwoods but mere saplings,
knocks over the wax,
snuffs the light to make way for the rotten stench
of his body, permeates his brain, kills fifty people
who are fat drunk on beer and bread all dressed
in costumes made to make fun of the walking dead.

Sleeping In Overdrive

Will Power

Ava threw rocks off the cliff, watched their dead weight sail off into the air. The wind caught them like a ball in a mitt. He gently handed them back to her the ones she needed to hold onto. They were all scuffed up, scarred in beautiful patterns of lines. Ava looked closely to see if they made any sense. She yelled out loud to the wind, "You are not the pitcher." The wind answered back to Ava, "No. You are the pitcher. I was giving you a second chance to stand back a little, take your time in choosing which rocks you wanted to keep."

Aya said, "These rocks are rocks. They are not mine to keep."

The air kindly whispered «You should not throw away what is not yours to begin with."

"What are they good for? To stub my toe?" she asked.

The wind whistled a tune Ava had heard before about wishing wells. She looked around and started stacking the rocks one by one around a big hole she found in the ground. When she was all done, she leaned over and made a wish. She heard the echoes repeat back something different. She thought her wish wouldn't come true and she kicked the rocks stubbing her toe every time. She picked up the loosened fallen rocks and set them on her newly formed wishing well. Pretty soon the wall was so high she could barely look into it. She found a boulder and pushed it up against the well, standing tall as if on a ladder. She heard it echo back the wish she had made: *please give me something I can hold onto.*

As she turned around to walk away and go about her day, she bumped into a large tree. She looked up at it and climbed all the way to the tip top. When she looked down she could see her wishing well had no bottom. It went straight through the ground and she could see the sea under the cliff. She thought how could it be a wishing well if it didn't have a bottom? How could it echo when it is bottomless?

The wind picked up and Ava heard it say, "Wishing wells are for you to do the work of making your dreams come true."

Sad and disappointed, she climbed back down the tree. She walked away with her head down not believing anything.

After a long while, her will to make her wishes come true overcame her. She returned to the wishing well on the cliff with a hole in the ground determined and defiant. There was a man standing there waiting.

"Do you need any help making a bottom for this wishing well?" asked the man.

She said, "Yes, my wishes keep going out to sea instead of the rocks", and she told him about what happened when she wanted to throw rocks.

He laughed and gave Ava a big hug. He said, "I am your wish."

She answered back angrily, "But you don't even know me."

He answered," I know you, I can see your fine work in how you stacked these rocks. Together we're going to make foundation for the well." He took her by the shoulders to stand back from the well and said, "See?"

Aya looked at the well. In big giant letters she saw the lines on the rocks had formed W – I – L – L.

He said, "My name is Will Power. What's yours?"

Slices of Bread without Butter

Unhappiness fattens as day turns into night.
Loneliness weighs heavier in silence.
Like the baby bird's beak,
the open mouth is still
hungry for words of love.
Adoration never filled the heart.
It was all only empty calories of sweetness,
the kind that turns the hurt of being left out into feeling full.

Note Left Behind

Detached
It's not true.
I can't be trusted when I say I love you.
It's not true my heart races when you are around.
It's not true how I think about you when you are not there.
Don't believe anything I say.

One day I will leave you out. ·
Forget you ever lived
in my soul hiding there like
a fresh passionate secret
adrenaline rush-only
you could ignite.
Don't believe anything I say.

Mountain Truth Hurts

Jagged edges tear my heart,
shoots through the palms of my hands,
empties my mind for a moment.
Reality pains the truth about things I didn't see.
I only felt the jagged edge,
touched the blade cutting the ties
to something that was never really there.

Spin Cycle

Cycle of the fish, the reptile, the bird.
The human being comes and goes.
Like teardrops falling from grace,

we recycle.

There is no such thing as forever
except in magazines
spewing bullets to make us run
to the makeup counter, the gym,
make us hide while we wait for the bad man
to go away.

Wake up to a new dawn, are we safe?
No one ever is.

I lost you in the mist of gray, somewhere between coming and going.
You were standing there with flowers and a smile while I kept pushing
uphill to win the battle of me against the machines
dispensing casings, soap,
cash at the ATM blows out

Leaves blow out, drop to the ground.
Dead scales float off molted feathers.
Twisted air wrung out to dry.
Pistol-whipped winds turn seasons
to the next show of color revolutions
reflected in oil made clean by agitation
going round and round.
Someday the revolvers will stop and the world will stop with it.

U - 10^9

The chemistry of sex is never without question as to who mixes
into me so that I dissolve into the hot flow of emotion that takes
over my will to say no and I cease to exist in the frame of mind the
person who should know better than to mix with the likes of U.
The U, who otherwise, lives worlds apart from me, and leaves
behind a film of residue that resides in my mind as if I am
wrapped in cellophane made to keep fresh for the next use.
I want to label it: Dangerous: May Explode Without Notice
because the only notice I had was when you approached and I
couldn't pull away from the draw of your number - the atomic
proof there was something there before it vaporized into the
colorless tube.

Ode to Two Chairs

There sit two chairs, side by side.
I sink into one, hold on to the
solid arms and back, lean back.
you in the other.

Marriage fell asleep on me.
It snored too loud, felt heavy.
I woke it up when I pushed it off
the edge of the space where I had
wanted to put a nice chaise lounge.
Now I dream without ever falling asleep.

Tilling the Brain Waves

The hermit sits on a calm sea of green lily pads
waiting for the red light to tell him go -
go where he can feel the nothingness of being alone
as the mist moistens his lips, refreshes the tear on his face,
surrounds his being like a veil.
No one knows he is color blind.
Can't see the difference between running
away into himself or standing in the middle of chaos.

The State of Sleeping

leaves me undisturbed
lets in the unknown of who is the real me
hidden just beneath the deepest layer of black.
She rises up to the surface in full color.
It is the art of learning how to mix
all that matters within the matter of gray and white.

Family Jewels

I am from a rock buried deep in dirt.
People look past all the pebbles
after the wave pulls it in,
moves it underneath heavy tides
to the other side of new shores,
untouched by those who will never know
what it is to be from the dregs
of the underworld disguised in richness
and wealth, poised in pleasantries
which force up what little is left
inside me to cut facets on the surface
and grind it down to sand.

The Milk Man's Daughter

lessens the weight of questions
held high on the balance beam,
adding little pebbles in the dish to
make things even in her head
over times he insisted *never lie.*
Each word got a pebble, flipping
through pages, listening to tales
of mothers in brothels and sons
playing in crawlspaces.
Stay quiet!

Dark walls covered in velvet
green paper stashed inside tins.
Little boy outside grows up
staring inside.
Strangers,
didn't care if they knew him.
Nobody did.
Lies poured out sweet
from his sisters and he –
denied remembering,
not even his dreams.

A moment's golden silence
buried the burden deeper.
Nothing learned except
how babies and a wife
made him an honest man.

Marble Eyes See Nothing

Cauliflower clusters of dried video brains
tested and scored in formaldehyde jars.
Rows upon rows of filled-in dots with #2 pencil,
carefully stacked, lined up and monitored by those who know
poverty endures as long as there's proof in all the tests.
Experiments gone wrong. Test tubes were cracked.
Little heads stuffed tight are ready for purging.

Love Story

A woman stood on the beach and threw out her boomerang.
It hasn't come back yet.

She's thrown two for sure she knew were authentic.
She's still waiting.

She's holding on to the third one, the one she knows is real.
She stands alone in love.

Mosaic Stars

I have five children with five homes.
We sit together in thick wide lines of grout.
Each broken shape of cobalt blue and
empty black, steel metal red, smoky purple
stands out against the chunky background.
On rainy days we let the water fill all the empty pots
that never bloomed any flowers. They split open.
The sharp pieces cut fingers and the rain rinses away the dust.

Fat Girl

gets swallowed up whole by lounging in pink pajamas on the couch.
She drinks powdered power drinks in between long hauls on the phone
bitching about how JoJo can never be the man she wants him to be.
Important afternoons are spent at the mall with long polished
nails gripping
the stroller in one hand as she moves through the plus sizes with
the other,
popping bubble gum while her little boy stares blankly at the tags
dangling.
Her clean hair is shiny and pulled back to show off the pretty
painted face
she sees in the rear view mirror as she drives home to serve herself
another
helping of French fries and a hamburger so she can fit in good with
what's on the television, flipping through the channels, tweeting all her
girlfriends about the saleswoman who gave her a dirty look when
she asked
why she wanted to return the item of clothing one size too small.

Happy Mother's Day

The news lady reported a story about a body found mutilated,
each piece severed from the core and hidden in the cushions
of an apartment belonging to a young man fresh out of college.
His eyes were found in the kitchen utensil drawer, each
finger tip was placed precisely on a shelf in the medicine cabinet.
The gruesome details were said to be committed by a suspected
felon just released from jail, but nothing had been confirmed.
The media flashed his picture in the hopes someone had seen him.
A woman watching her TV saw the mug shot and said, "My son."
She picked up her phone as it rang. Not knowing whether to answer
she put it down and went to the back bedroom to pull out
baby pictures of when they celebrated his 2nd birthday at
a McDonald's, just the two of them. They were so happy then.

Staining the Sheets

The blood soaked through the mattress.
The fibers could not hold it all. It worked its way down
into the inner lining where it will remain until cut open
when it is thrown into the dumpster.
The middle, caught on a sharp metal corner,
exposes fluff that held your stained secret of
how you never wanted to stop saturating the sheets
with your presence on top of me, under me, beside me.
The hardness of your lust pushed into me deep,
pierced through my heart, made a tiny hole, at first.
Tiny droplets of blood outlined the undetectable
realization I was lying in a comfortable bed of lies.
The stain was nothing more than a wet spot of your cum
embedded in the coils of my soul making the delineation
clear it would be discarded as no longer useful.
My heart cried out for something more than to be fooled
from the inside of what was once a restful place to sleep.
The mattress has been replaced with a much firmer one.
The salesman told me it was stain-resistant.
I bought it anyway.

Clips of You

In the back of my mind, you're there knowing
where the good places are to hide,
stay safe until the night comes when I see your eyes open
as mine close the door to the noises of the day.

The movie plays a different ending I never watch.
The sun rays reached in and pointed you out,
startled you back into the corner,
and the light shines bright while you're there
reading the back of my mind, knowing the end.

Who's He Fooling?

"Elect me, I am the man," who is going to -what?
Make me want to curl up and die like a pill bug
found in the corner of my patio and swept up
with the rest of the dirt the wind blew in?
Pointing out current laws about how to live and
what is right as if laws were here before earth itself.
Laws change, rules change, I grow old and watch
the curtain billow in and out as the figures
change the set for another compelling scene
of big heads luring little dogs with fake plastic biscuits.
Who is he fooling?
Oh yes, that old man who believes every word written
by someone else in the playbook. It's there. Must be true.
He might have to change the route he drives to work,
might have to change living life bent on a little bench
praying for someone else to bring him that plate of
fruit plastered in gold when the bugs have eaten their
fair share and are no longer hungry and crying for more.

Hat on a Hot Head

No one knows who lives there
in the mansion on the hill
with its empty cement faintly bleached
People want to be known as unknown.
Anonymous puts them way up high
above the riff raff as if
Holly Wood herself is living in satin sheets
unyielding to the crowds
yelling in the streets, *more, more, more.*
They'll read all about him in slick lines
written to entertain but never tell
how he lives like the homeless person
who forgot who he was,
before society took over, took away his soul -
and people say they want to be like him
Don't say a word about who you are, what you think,
just drive and look pretty.
You'll be first in line for the identity card that reads:
M T High. 2 Good Foya St. Ignore Everyone, USA
Even some movie stars take a stance but you can't
because anyone you don't know, doesn't matter,
and being private means you're better than
the same human being who wants to make their
life blank, would give a million dollars
to start over, wash it in the same bleach
you use to rinse the walls in your house
to get rid of the staleness you breathe out.
One day the dirt will fall out from under
the foundation, give way to the heavy
burden of keeping it all locked up and safe.
And we'll all read about it in the media how
this person no one knew looks just like you -
the man who broke down one day,

Patricia Youngs

went berserk running in between all the cars
cruising the strip yelling his name and address.
We all showed up, took pictures of the fancy columns
covered in mud, windows broken, curtain pulled back
so we could all enjoy the show of what it's like to
live inside your private life.

Population Overgrowth

Five fingers reach out
like the fly touches
a piece of crusty bread,
presses down -
Is the mattress firm?
Will she like
soft pillows, lights on?
Her voice comes stealthily
behind me, I jump.
My hands turn around
grab her, fingertips
touch skin silky soft,
propagation begins
and the eggs hatch clean
hands, body, and soul.

Corner Store Dog

Dog smiles abound at my house, paws padding
coming to give me their nose in my face,
soft tongue kisses on my chin as I forget
the water running in the backyard,
the fat man sitting pretty
while the starving man lies hungry
and the dogs continue panting satisfactorily
after a round of tug of war played with an origami rope
made of twisted dollar bills.
My friend told me it wasn't right
I let my dog play with money like that
at which I laughed and said yes, they enjoy
playing with other people's money.
My dog heard me talking, came over, stood next to me,
wanted to be patted on the head and told he was good boy.
I don't think there is a dog in the world that won't give you his smile,
a slight bow of his head when he knows a person loves him.
Dogs offer a smile to a stranger. I like to smile at dogs.

Impromptu Rehearsal

When the words come rushing out of my mouth
and I can't stop talking about what I know,
And what I know is probably something you don't want to hear;
When the words are already spoken, already said,
the impression is there, impressed on your mind that I am
a freak, something alien that doesn't relate,
and the curl of your lip says I am ugly. I am sinister. I am dirty.
I am not who you expected when I smiled graciously, legs pressed
together.
You thought I might be someone dainty with manners and I am…
except I told you everything you ever wanted to know and now it's
like
you know too much and there's no room to play up the first act.
I wanted to skip over it, get to the real you, but you were in your
makeup.
I went back to the dressing room and took the star off my door.

Flip and Flop

Flip can't breathe, her gills are stiff. Look into her eye,
clear light golden staring back at me stiff like a board.
Freeze-dried. Land locked. Throw her back where she came from.
Into the shade. Moisture lingers in the air. She does a flip.
Flop catches her in the deep end where they gulp residue from oil
floating on top. They slip down in the dark, lost in the seaweed.

Dear Grandpa (I'll Never Tell)

how I hear of other people talk about grandfathers.
I wished I knew you but I didn't
because you were someone I never knew until I was too old.
And if you were still around I think I could hear you say:
Come here little one I want to tell you a story.
No need to sit on my knee, I'm flat out on the street
claiming name to your daddy and his sisters –
well I hope they marry well, if they're lucky.
I'm doubled over, head between my knees,
people walked on past as an obstacle in the street.
- and the woman you call mother goes by another name
I'll never tell. I was busted up crawling before you ever did.
There are no pictures to show you proof of how I lived.
You might hear it from a second cousin of a second cousin
And if you're sorry you never knew me, It's just as well.
The rest is just heresay about how the story ends.
The "just know it was a happy" was for the school year book.
Dear Granddaughter, I don't want you to know me all wrapped
on the street with a bottle and blanket. Just keep living
like you never knew me. There's nothing to tell.

Scratch Ticket

Standing in line to buy pots and pans, soap to wash hands,
Clean meat from teeth. Logging in for a flash of pixels, dots,
stare at the ceiling, pages of sex on the screen, give a round of
applause.
People declare in the streets, in a pulpit, on bathroom walls in
black markers,
I was here.
There's money to be made wearing them clothes in the right size
and color.
Stand back,
I don't want you to see the holes I haven't filled in.

Wasted Wax Offerings

Eyes from the other side see moths flutter
to beats of flickering echoes from candles' fire
as darkness looms in the middle of day.
There is no meaning at the end of the line
without the question mark. The soldier blinds himself
with pages too thin to cover promises only made
when the book lies open.
The wind tells the truth,
whispers it in delicate melodies heard by the birds
nestled in branches during the lull between bombs.
Sand blows thick through air, the eyes cannot read,
the book gets ripped, and the birds pick up the pages,
make their nests, arrange them in between old
pieces of wax and dead moths found on the ground.

Freedom Cell

divides and multiplies from the confines of the mind.

Heartless mind reaches in the prison cell at the compound, pulls
out a twig tangled
In a pile of branches cut down to see the clouds move across
the sky.

The twig is examined as sufficient support to hold up deteriorating
walls put up to block
the sun, the moon, the air, to suffocate those deemed unworthy of
happy smiles from watching little hands play with wagging puppy
dog tails.

Freedom rings through small holes of torn cloth used to wrap
the wounds of soiled minds living in dark streets, long stretches
of cement put down so progress could roll through faster, more
efficiently than the weight of a man's body at the bottom of his soul.

It yearns to hold him up, give him the footing to climb the trunk,
crawl out along the strongest branch, stand up with no hands,
look down at the world full of little ants, look up with closed eyes,
let loose his mind to find his heart as the wind blows away the dirt
after the soul has been pulled out of deep wet mud.

It wants to dry the teardrops, let the muck fall away, reveal its true
colors as they fall back down into the earth, reseed itself, grow
into a new tree, small twigs and all. Grow roots in fertile soil to
give back to earth what earth created out of tiny synapses full of
hopeful survival.

Like the sea turtle born in the sand as it crawls to swim in the sea;
the mind wants to be free.

Lava Monster

I held my hand out, looked you in the eye,
there was hesitation in the air that night
we stood close. I wanted you to like me.
But instead you turned and walked away.
My hands return to neutral position.
My heart covered in soot still flickering
a tiny bit in the red hot middle
throws out sparks that extinguish on landing.

Dinner Bell

If I were president sitting in my white house, each Friday night of
the week I'd ask my spouse to pass the peas at a dinner table set
for twelve-

twelve thugs, twelve CEO's, twelve teenagers, twelve illegal
immigrants, twelve lobbyists, twelve teachers, twelve of everyone
from all parts of society, filthy, rich and filthy rich, fifty times
in all to represent the fifty states of confusion, arrogance, deceit,
happiness, security, defiance, rebellion, conformity, hunger,
production, mourning, euphoria before the apocalypse.

The only hidden agenda would be the destination. The invitees
taken hostage, blindfolded by surprise from behind, wrists tied
with rope. They wouldn't know they were going to break bread,
share wine, create an evening of no barriers with no masks for
more hours in a day and a night when the moon gets stuck and
doesn't move until reset by bats flying in the sun.

My white house would be set in the deep woods, hidden behind a
thick forest of trees, a cloud of smoke piping out of the chimney.
There would be a big pot of honey warmed over a fire in a grand
fireplace as we ate sweet baby meat served to us on silver platters.

"Please have some olives, picked fresh from my tree." As olives are
passed everyone would know how to converse with ease. Music
would be heard by the trees and they'd sway back and forth
with the wind applauding the great president who knew how to
please each person's heart with comfort and grace despite painful
restraints.

The lull of conversation would be filled with my voice asking each
what they are doing, how they are doing, if they've any plans for

the future. "Please tell me your story of working in such and such place or perhaps that wooden cane all covered in lace?"

I'd take it in all their words, have them written on paper, spray painted on walls overlaying murals of mushroom clouds over mutated beings my country has created along its way to stardom, flying on stardust, on its way to the moon. It left me behind to counsel the last of a dying race. I would cease to rule.

And so if I were president, at the beginning of the week, I'd be happy to retire to my bedroom with the sound of the bell, go rest, and never wake up.

One Serving Recommended Daily

I make too much out of orgasmic muscles.
I feed myself the sweet delicacy of heat exploding into fire.
Make a feast out of the juices that spill warm over the brim.
They satiate my palate for the euphoric rush when the knife
pushes in, opens up, takes the meat to my lips.

Haiku

hope rises within.
open minds behind closed doors.
slit of light peers out.

Tanka

Late night lovers meet
Her body gives rise to his
Clean sheets cover them
Sleep leaves the room fast
Forbidden sex reigns supreme
Happiness trumps jealousy

Recipe for Snowflake Cake

Mix two parts sifted reasoning with one part wild hair
picked fresh from a garden high up in a cloud.
Add ten drops of tears to every half smile that comes
out of the box labeled Insecurity.
Mix together thoroughly until it resembles one big mess.
Get out the bag of crushed hearts, pick out the biggest one,
wrap in a piece of old news and place in the middle
of said mess until it resembles a big happy cake complete
with dreamy piping and thick sweet frosting.
Batter will be lumpy so use your imagination of what resembles happy.
Make filling and frosting of your choice, but not vanilla.
Adding vanilla will only ruin the unique character of what's inside.
Bake thoroughly and as often as necessary.
Pay no attention to all the smoke -
it's part of the process that goes into the processor.
You'll need a big apron to catch all the splatter.
After you're done creating and there's nothing
but Me standing in front of you, we'll go down
to the local bar and have ourselves a toast to
the craftiest, tastiest people-maker recipe ever written.

Unrequited Love

The walls echoed your voice
and I heard vibrations hum
a tune the birds knew by heart.
They heard you were coming
and the house grew warm,
threw open its arms when
you walked through the door,
moved your finger along smooth
walls covering the different
colors lying beneath stark white.
You were the one who mixed
the bluest blue into crystal clear
drops of rain dripping down
the walls in a winter storm,
smearing the high gloss shine
with the palms of your hands,
and you molded the walls
with the pain of feeling lost
sleeping between sheets that
smelled of us after the sweat dried.

Truth

Time inside myself
watches who I am
on the outside as I walk
on past. my reflection
catches wrinkles in my skin,
my clothes, my lies.
Three dimensional
between points of
valor, sadness, strength.
The sun shines gold rays
on ashes in the ground,
branding it a solid bar
of history from my heart.

Sovereign Souvenirs

Instructions for My Son's Art Project

Cut it out along the edges, careful not to tear the middle, the
inside of the artichoke, the heart of
diamonds, of an eagle flying in the land of the lost minds stuck on red.
Roll out the scissors in all its steel-plated splendor, pointy tips too
sharp for small hands.
Shred it into oblivious snow sparkles falling like dust in the
middle of summer.
Fold it up and hold it open for all to see the connected dots
dashing for play dough worms in their
hidden box of secret tales landed by fairies on dragon tails held
high as you stand by waiting
for the last train to Phoenix.

Cup of Joe

Awake with my cup of Joe, I see an eagle in darkness. Little
sunshine caused the eagle to bleed.
I write the middle name Joe, Joseph, stuck in between father and
son with nothing to call his own.
An ER doc saved my life one night. We shared the same
ambulance in the crash of '32.
Like shooting stars, kangaroos from the other side of midnight
went flashing by.
"Is that a question or a statement," asks the Dragnet man. I notice
the dragonfly on his shoulder.
"That's not what you think. It's a parrot in disguise."

Printed in Mo Jo

Untitled 1

If I could see the sparkle fluttering by the top of your head when you wished me a thousand kisses in the dark and the dog stories were all written for me like the daisy petals pulled off one by one as you sat on the grass in the morning sun with your head down wondering how it would be to have the tip of my tongue trace the lines of your cheeks in that secret hidden place only you knew about.

Untitled 2
When I go back, I can't go forward, and when I go forward there is nothing there except the same dream of how I know you from a past life full of force and glory without a face or a name, like the nothing there standing behind me, in front of me. It was in that house I felt you there beside me for a flashing moment, so real, I went to open the door and all I saw was a lightning storm ripping through the night sky. Do you remember? They all said he played the piano.

Extra! Extra! Pope Sells Out

Lady Jay and Bertha are sitting side by side getting pedicures and catching up on Lady J's news.

Lady Jay: He never left me.

Bertha: Intoxicating, isn't it?

Lady Jay: He never left me for reasons I don't know. He stayed secret and knew all of mine.

Bertha: They say love never sleeps. Maybe it was love that he watched over you like that.

Lady Jay: I gave him his watch back.

Bertha: What was it?

Lady Jay: It was a silent one. You could sleep with it and never hear the ticking against your ear at night.

Bertha: A digital one, then.

Lady Jay:It could have been. It was disguised as a wind up one though. It looked antique.

Bertha: A fake then.

Lady Jay: Perhaps, yes. Fake love, fake watch. But my secrets were never fake.

Bertha: Secrets never are. Makes the pope look good.

Lady Jay: Didn't make me look very good.

Bertha: Depends on who you are. Are you the kind who goes giving the pope what he wants?

(A moment of silence lapses. Bertha picks up a magazine.)

Bertha: Look at this, says here the pope sold out. He sold his confessions to The Onion.

Lady Jay: What? I never knew a priest to let loose like that. Let me see that.

(Bertha hands her the article)

Lady Jay: Says they're changing pope's title to Hope instead of Pope. That capital P was supposed to stand for the people. We don't have that any more.

Bertha: Gotcha...all we have is pure genuine hope now.

Brown Colored Crayons

My momma had two brown eyes she used to watch
her two brown children playing in the brown dirt.

She wore a brown dress cinched at the waist with a big bow in the back
pew at church on Sundays.

She saw a big brown man who looked like her husband get into a
Cadillac, all long and brown, engine running.

It had a black top and racy chrome wheels loaded with gangster
guns in the trunk no one could see 'cept for momma.

She ran into the house calling our names, wiped her hands on
her apron before tossing it aside, grabbed a suitcase full of money
from the top shelf behind the empty tequila bottles she saved for
decorative memories when they made me.

We went out the back door all holding hands, running together,
ducked our heads when we heard the bullets shatter the windows.

We ran for our lives, blood rushing under our skin as we found
shelter in the house of a white dog in the middle of the yard.

No one was home and the dog didn't bark when we opened the
door and saw the note on the table:
Please come in. I'm hurt and unable to
see you in the dark of my light-hearted
mind.

She came out of the bedroom and said, "I can only see in shades of
brown,
would like to sit down? You are the only people I've seen since the day

they took my sweet children away. They promised them rolls of gold ribbons unraveled in the bottom of a river, lured them into cold water when I knew they could not swim."

Momma said we could hug her and the old lady started crying when she said she could see again.

All it took was the mixing of crayons on skin.

Deaf and Blind

There is love in between the blank spaces of time when we think
there is nothing going on.
It reaches out sometimes like a crying baby fills the room with the
sound of wanting.
And sometimes it is so quietly invisible we believe it isn't there.
There is love in between screams calling names to deaf ears.
An angel smears her red paint on their faces to disguise it.

Where Charlie Was Born

Dark words swirl in my head and out they come from my mouth
like a flock of flies.
They fill the room with black and you can hear their wings
buzzing. Their eyes
become my eyes and I see everything in all the facets, each one a
different view.
Each one a reasonable rage on how I have been duped into
believing what is not true.
Each one taking my sight making me blind to the sun shining and
the quiet color of flowers.

A girl is waiting there in a field of green, always young. She died
many years ago before I was born.
She wants to tell me the secrets of the flies but I can't hear her. She
waits patiently and with such hope.
One day we'll fly away to Amsterdam, land in the middle of the
night, and we'll see the tulips.

Poised Sugar For Sale

There were M and M's in the zucchini bread
Like water in the toilet, sweet smelling violets
On a rainy day in the dead winters I longed for
When the farm toys went missing under the tree.
Hey you, said the horse pulling the carriage as I
Walked alongside him, turned to give him a
Carrot, an apple. He gave me a sly look that said
little mares eat oats and lambs eat ivy.

Williamesque Skipping Down Memory Lane
With That Story From Oh, Didn't Know

Kellogg's Tide with the Arm & Hammer at his side turning the
tables upside down cards two by two fools fooled you blue chips
on chipped shoulders of soldiers who sold her the soldered blankets
on bare feet big bellies hung in the shower with father in the motel
room rubbing the hood over at the storage station altercation alter
the bus at the altar hooked horns on the walking sticks push the
sheep poke the pig deep in the hip, hip, hippie chick little chicks
all yellow with pigeon poop on the side baby ducks drowned in
the sink with the air all dry sucked clean like the plastic bag on
the face say blue baby blue blue-chip stock stuck soup bull ropes
at the blue chip poker table owned it like the harp on the hill. I
dream in green no dollars holla girls cry one at a time never die
never lasting lest the sting get you in between the miracle whip
whose the boss if Malcolm is in the middle and there's no last
dance for black slippers on the jane who married uncle luck down
at the newsstand for two heads are better than one always that
same old jock joke what the hell I'll pay you for it. Vans down at
the wonder bread hailing cabs called smokey and black keys and
darkie don't you know clowns don't pay for cover charges on his
white steer following the stallion in the stall yelling her name,
many names, don't know who any more for the fight in the back
alley with coat hangers lashing on guard! So very slippery in the
oily slik don't fall don't scream timber lassie will never come she's
under the bridge saving the drowned horse swimming upstream
racing the canoe and the snow shoe down yonder past the red bard
and the red door and all the churches pining for trees. No wind.
Star fires take flight broad daylight with red eyes closed on the all
nighter to nowhere. Nothing but nothing she said. Yeah nothing
all right. Save me the pie so I can throw on fair day on the fairway
drive to rainbow land and ice land and grace land in the lands of
the bland sideways sidecar. Ride big rides for me as we go round
the sweet merry go round over the hill and through the woods

of iron and steel stealing my breath away took your breather pills poured them down the sink turned pink on a Friday night. Keeper keep her she's a save her on that knight kings crossed horses switched the trade for shade. Savior sweet savior where will be Ju jus go? How many words does it take to lick the lollipop circus 464 and counting like crows squawk wishing they were hawks. Hocked the land on the sunrise, tequila they say to kill ya they say, no no no just dancing at mid night on the mid way.

Polar Bear with a Heart-Shaped Brain

Third floor down lived a polar bear. She lived two lives inside
her two brains shaped like a heart. People called her the bipolar
bear and they taught her to ride her bi-cycles in the circus for all
to enjoy. She entertained the masses on Sundays and the third
Friday of every month. "Come see the heart-shaped white bear"
read the marquee on the front of her apartment building. One
day a teacher came to sit with her in her bedroom away from all
the crowds. He taught her pedagogy and said she should never
perform for humans again. That people should know better than
to be entertained by such a special bear as she. He moved her out
of the third floor down apartment and into an ice cave that floated
on an sice berg in Greenland. The newspapers printed a story
about how she escaped her prison. The teacher laughed and wrote
the editor about the typo. He said it was a prism, not a prison,
the heart-shaped polar bear lived in. Her heart turned diamonds
when she died. There were 21 perfectly cut facets. It was the most
beautiful prism anyone had ever seen. The autopsy reported they
melted from her heart-shaped brain down to her heart when
she reached Greenland. It concluded she lived the truest of true
minds – with an empty brain and heavy heart.

Devil S Muse

I am the devil
No, I am the devil and you are my muse.
And he danced to a beathless beat.
I am dead.
No, I am death and you are my breath.
And she danced to invisible heat.
I am life.
No, I am love and you are my heart
I am an angel
No, I am dressed in black
And they danced in a moonless street

Getting to the World Race on Time

Spirits soar through the air, invisibly claiming unrivaled power of light
spread a billion miles into space to kiss stars, all of them in the seconds
the pallbearers reach the dead's destination and a baby's head for air.
They comfort me, wrap around me like a warm blanket, usher me
through
the revolving doors flapping, flapping always flapping. Hear it.
Take a step in.
Move around my pied-off section, around this little piece of earth,
grounded,
pushing against the clear heavy glass. Take a look around, round
and round.
Step off, stand still, listen to them soar, listen to their silent grace
filling space.
Jet engines line up for take-off ready to race against timeless
wings; they will not win.

Indentation of finger pokes on my skin.
I didn't feel them at first.
Didn't know they were there.
Then I saw the fingerprints.
They made my skin crawl
with bugs from the bottom of the pot
at the bottom of the hill,
behind the mountain, past the forest,
way past the forest in a field of rainbow grass.
Where they're born, I guess.
They crawled in the circled crevices printed on my skin.

I lifted them and set them up to the lab.
She identified, confirmed, licked them off the slide
and then ate them. Said they're the best
delicacy searched by chefs for the past hundred years.
Who touched you, she asked.

I said I didn't know, but I felt the pressing in every nerve
of my body and then I saw them crawl up the walls.
They spelled my name and then they wrote:
We Love You
That's when I collected each one by one by one by one....

Lady Duck and Mister Goose

The dusty town sold out on lines,
wanted a stab with their fork tines
at a piece of their heart-shaped meal
while she sipped champagne with a seal
shared fried potatoes with no eyes
out on the dock loaded with rocks.

Little Dog on a Full Moon

With his uncombed wiry hair and little tongue lopped to the side
he jumped and he jumped and he ran and he ran like a crazy
hellion on wheels going to race the wind on a calm full moon night.
Hey there little guy, I said, as he flew on by me wondering how tasty
my apple pie would be, waiting for me, when we got home sweet home.
But my little dog didn't wait for me as he ran and ran and jumped
into the night.
I lost him I thought. This is it. He finally caught up with that
invisible wind.
I looked all around, at the park, at the playground, behind the
alley and then
I looked up, ready to ask a favor from his guardian angel when
what did my eyes
See? But my little wiry, happy tongued dog up dancing on the top
of a round full moon.
He looked down at me, skipping and hopping and wagging his
tail, gave a few yaps at me.
I heard him clear as that full moon night say, Come on up, silly
person, it's happy up here.
I thought how could this be? I looked down at the ground where I
just buried him full of tears.
I said back to him, It's okay little guy. You keep dancing. I'll catch
you at the next full moon.

All Caterpillars are Free

Tis to the future I look up with swollen red eyes.
My breath steadies in the shade of a shadow
pressed against the wall of muddy sand packed dry,
I see the round cone of a castle holding up in the wind.
A man appears as if the wind pushed him there.
Don't cry, he tells me. I say, why not, and wipe my nose.
Hold out your hand, he instructs. Puts a wriggly caterpillar
in the middle of my palm. I feel its tiny legs crawl along,
searching for a leaf up my arm. It reaches my shoulder,
then my neck, up my cheek, checks the snot dripping
off my lip. I feel it step up on my eyelashes onto my lid,
over my eyelid. Across my eyebrow, it finds a spot
in my hairline just above my ear. I hear it tell me its name.
"Gratis, pleased to meet you," I whisper back.
Taking his hand in mine, I ask which way to the trees?
Pointing to a large piece of driftwood, he says, that's all there is.

Girls Who Talk to Too Much

I didn't want to cry but when I read your words
I could see your face and it reminded me of me.
Just like you, I too, run fast thoughts like the
imperfections of daisies with missing petals.
We pulled them off as we ran through open
fields, happy with such excitement our fingers
blindly grabbed at whatever we ran by.
We are insignificant by other standards,
the rushing of words like the water running
down gutters children play in after the rain.
You remind me that Patty's words count in the
unbrushed mornings of gala evenings spent out
on the balcony talking up the time, speaking to my heart,
smoking cigarettes with short nails and chipped polish,
drinking in the wine of wishes we knew were ours.

Mother at Midnight

She's full of maggots, not worth eating,*
Spinning round on the spindle
Which way is north?
Is she perfectly round?

Yes, she is. Beautiful. Full and complete,
Keeps giving and taking around the sun.

She is as beautiful as the sun so bright.
And when the maggots reach her head
She'll show you how the moon rises
Through the trees and over mountains.

Stand still and watch birds fly.
Sit next to the vines, watch her grow.

The maggots made whales deaf.
They died singing her song.
The wind echoes it now and then.
Did you hear it?
Was it as beautiful as She?
* from the movie version of The Hobbit

Of a Bird I Never Met

Only left little hints
he was around, round
zomewhere, playing
with me, my mind,
my sanity, my soul.
I paw at the air but
there's nothing there
not even a bird.

Perennial Sketches of Me, pantoum

I want to be a flower
pressed in between pages
of words gone by in spring.
I shall not wither dry.

Pressed in between pages,
preserve my petals under shade.
I shall not wither dry
from summer basking lazy

Preserve my petals under shade
until winter comes again.
From summer basking lazy
bookmark where we left our prints.

Until winter comes, again
pages waxed of fragile stems
bookmark where we left our prints.
I want to be a flower printed in your heart.

Flower Shop, dialogue

Woman: Oh Dear Sir, I'd like to return these flowers.
Clerk: What's the matter with them? I need to enter a reason in the box, is all.
Woman: They're black. They turned black as soon as I got them home.
Clerk: Okay, turned black. What color were they?
Woman: They were white, and they were supposed to turn grey. The clerk examined the returned goods.
Clerk: Looks like you bought the fluorescent glow in the dark ones. See this tag?
Woman: Tag? Where?
The woman peered into the flowers to look for it.
Clerk: It's here. Kind of small, but at the base where the green stops.
Woman: Hmm…one would need a magnifying glass to see that. Why so small?
Clerk: I don't know. Maybe it's meant to be seen with newborn eyes.
Woman: What?
Clerk: Well, if our vision decreases as we age, then when we're first born, we can see everything, even the tiniest tag like this one.
Woman: A glow-in-the-dark flower for a baby? Who would want that?
A man enters the flower shop and overhears the conversation.

My Cousin It

It is a mingle of creativity with a dark side, say an oatmeal stout with bright streamers pouring out the top. One can say it is the stout that doesn't belong or that the streamers don't belong. Either way, the two are combined and visible and talked about, pondered over and then forgotten. Or not. Might come up again by chance in the rain or a dream or never at all.

Little Stream of Consciousness from a Greatly Delusional Firecracker

There are places to hide and places to ride. I'll take them all on a little square map wrapped and folded inside my knapsack along with my flashlight and lighter to light up the dark spots when I can't see right or think right and I hide in the dark alleyway hoping against hope no one can see me, but they will. when they do, I'll hop on a cable car or a bus or a bike or whatever I can find to go for a ride. Ride far far away to the sea shore where the sun may or may not be out, but it'll be there and I won't want to hide from it any more. I mean really, who can hide from the sun? Well I did. for months and months I stayed inside my house with my robe over my clothes just in case someone saw me I would say I was sick. Because the sun didn't want to talk to me nor shine on me, nothing. I thought we were in a fight or something but I didn't recall how it started in the first place. I hid and I thought and I thought about what and how it happened the sun stopped shining on me. I wanted to know that when I saw him again, we'd be cool and I'd get all hot and happy right away knowing the fun in the sun was the truth and nothing else.

Roses in an Open Window

My windows are open like my heart is to you. You just have dodge
the spit from decrepit spaces between my teeth, the little bits
of filth that come flying from my gut. Because my heart stands
wavering in the wake of the onslaught. I'd give you my own sword
and shield if I could, but I think mine are too small or you are too
big. However, my heart's full room capacity is more than enough.
It has to be a carriage full of roses I have stored in it.

Post Landing Questionnaire

Did you fly with a different name?
Hold on and pull up before leaping?
Were you strong in the middle?
Did the layers fall away?
Yes, like a sparkling pink tutu
from the highest point, it flew.
X _Olga Zeeland_

For April, acrostic

Perhaps truth stood dormant in the execution
To sound down partitions to my brain.
Soaked, drenched, pattern-triggered thoughts
Drain a parched sister's dying memories.

Whisking away eggs of golden seeds
Into the spring air on a windless night.
Listen to them dance in the moonlight
Leaning on each other in a straight line.

Noon heat cooks them even and hot.
Oven timer ticking away in the kitchen
Tapping out the final pop of the last kernel.

Damn the routine sounds pounding my
Ears, ringing the alarm bells I
Smashed with a hammer swinging hard
To make the words tell the story of how
Rich dirt feels between my finger and thumb.
Over the rainbow never felt so close in the
Year of the horse's tale.

May I please, with my dirty face and weathered hands,
Excuse myself from tripping over the line.

Missionary Rapist Frac King

The sky reflected in the oily puddle at my feet
and air exhaled quickly in shallow breaths
trying to avoid the noxious gas -
I hang up the pump, pumping gallons into
exhausting, living, breathing life,
under the engine, the beautiful glorious hood,
choking bees, burrowed missionary style,
hauled hoses latch on
in the middle of the night;
the calm before the blast.

I look down at my feet,
see slick edges glazing back at me, iridescent,
shale-shaped, chipped, fractured,
popped out and landed from the injection
like a needle in my knee to make the pain go away.
Find the sweet spot,
rejoice in the money, the jobs,
the force of humans on nature
to bring up her orgasmic richness,
reached in long and imaged
like the million dollar baby's vomit I am standing in.

Apple Tree in December

Walking the lane, a man and his boy
lay down their guns and their toys.
The man thought he'd be clever
jumps up a big tree with a lever
from his boy's bruised knees. Says,
"I'll be Jack, just you stand back,
Keep your nose out of trouble."

Shaking the tree, the worms drop out.
Little kid stands below opens his mouth
thinks it is rain. Old man laughs, coughs,
spits out a serpent, head slithers down
around his neck. Little boy watches
his face turn blue, then purple and
he holds out his tongue hoping to catch
his eyes. "Mmm..." thought the boy,
"That was double good."
And he caught the last worm with the
shape of his cap remembering his old man
always loved to say he'll turn blue into the sky.

He walked on alone and when he got home
no one was there but old mama on the stairs
staring at the walls as if she was in a stiff scare.
"Don't you worry," said the boy grabbing his toy,
"Papa's gone blue just like he knew he would.
We can dance in the fire deep in the wood,
let the smoke catch the tip of his hood,
and we'll light him up like Christmas joy."

Autumn Leaves Glitter Notes

Crackling leaves,
like dried paper laid down in the sun too long,
words faded,
and the crunch, crunch, crunching
meshes down into teeny bits of nothing,
blows away in the wind.
Fine handmade linen starched white,
tore up and cracked like little bits of my heart spread wide,
scatters the air, sprinkles the soul with glitter,
nestles the mind into the quiet comfort of dark,
Attempts to leave me unearthed, flapping in the wind
brought you back to the sunlit pile glistening shiny red and gold.
Swishing the dew drops fallen after the wind cried
over silence
too beautiful for words, you held me close,
brushed the hair from my face
saw the glitter come dancing from my eyes.

Numbing Circus

There is a pain in my window seat. Humiliation dances through
the nose ring of a bear. All the rings are chained together. Do
the money chain dance. And then men act like hungry monkeys
watching bananas and fancy fruit go by on a string. We are all in
the cage throwing coins down hill. Hey, man do a wheelie for me -
through fire with your butt cheeks glued down and your hands
tied to bare metal handle bars so I see the heat come screaming
through your eyes a I watch from my window, throw money
at your pain. Confetti pours in the street and the bear cannot
breathe, can't smell fear nor honey, stands next to the chained
elephant with the naked girl on his back. Can you see their glass
eyes? Aren't they pretty? They can dance, do tricks. There are the
ponies tied to the spinning pole. Their heads held high by halters
all day. The chain is too tall for short legs. Nose up!! $1 pony
ride and no one's in line. Rusty lunch boxes left out in the rain.
Everyone traded a ticket worth $10 for a movie.

Dance to an Invisible Backdrop

I saw black birds playing in the wind
Like lottery power balls darting sideways,
kites with no strings, just my eyes
And this pen to write it down.

Bats Eat Bugs

Kill from the right, burn, murder, hatchets on fire.
There are ten thousand hammers in my shed.
To run and talk at the same time brings the bats out.
Silent lift after fair warning comes swiftly as they
fly blindly in dark caves. What will they know when
there is no sound? The bats, they are thousands,
one for each hammer, hang together on the wall.
Will the bugs still watch and listen from dark corners?

Beware if all sirens alarm when you approach.
Even you may not be welcome when the doors
are locked. I do not like to live in a closed box.
All dark with only my own murderous light to
shine on the bugs you have in your pocket.

Oh, but the pockets rest on the body of you
who can teach bats to lie down full from
the meal you had ready for them in your hand
In your pocket.

This box is not a box and I am not blind nor deaf.
Do not presume all my false starts at the gate
means I am such in a hurry to see you.

Someday there will be no more chatter of bugs and bats.
I would ask what then, knowing there's a knife in my pocket,
There's no point when all corners appear vanished in the sunlight.
No point to remembering when I tore away a back entrance,
clawed with my own hands like an animal insisting there was
something there on the other side.

Can You Hear Me Now

soaring above ocean waves of my brainstorms,
washing away the good-byes through your head
swirling, looking at me in the sky,
singing songs, piercing your heart. Little daggers
land upon your tongue and you hear my silence
in the breezes, in the wet flowers at dawn,
a baby's first breath unnoticed in white blankets.

Can you hear me now underneath all the noise?
Whispering, pleading for you to come to me,
play with me in the light, dance in the wake
of death's funeral on top of hot stoves steaming
with dishes of bread pudding swollen in the middle
from the pushing of carts and the brakes in line
with each other head to head, ear to ear, mouth to mouth

Can you hear me now with your eyes wide open to see
the dragons come swooping down skimming the waves.

Carnal Earthlings Are Hungry - Pantoum

Dig deep into the sun
my little one.
Two fours on the floor.
Epiphanies open doors.

My little one,
say the word, language unknown.
Open-door epiphanies
herd you into the wool.

Say the word language, unknown
soldier dies in flight,
herds into the wool.
Dig deep into the sun.

Children of the Fire

Feed man's brain corpses and meat. Earth's children will grow.
Light is not innocent. It shines on death of unconscionable acts.
Fingers point. And the judgment crew stands guard
in fields of flowers and wheat during the moment
of crushing bones between teeth.
To catch a child's flame is fruitless.
The apple fell in your hand.
Savor the juice while time dissipates your eyes
when the sun shifts in the blink, casts twisted shadows
of characters laid out against a crooked fence.
Black on white melts the colors, burns them into the disco ball
twirling round and round, reflects the mirrors in your mind
when children dance to the beat of fire's laughter and grace.

For Winter Solstice 2013 - Sestina

In the darkness
comes a snow-covered hush
from deep inside the forest.
The wanting of my soul
by the moon at midnight
drawn by a line from outer space

pulls the inner space
between light and dark
nestled under fallen leaves. A knight's
shining white horse could hush
the wind with his soul
stomp prance, make his foe

rest on bended knee for esters
to fill his nostrils, make space
to breathe in the winter sol-
stice on this dark
hour of snow-covered hush.
My eyes see the black knight

riding a white horse in the night
through the snow-covered green forest.
I say," Don't cry, hush, hush
the spell of tears falling in space
that holds hands with stars in the dark-
ness of my soul.

There is great light in soul-
itude of this star-filled night
midway between heaven's dark
sky and this wintergreen forest
laid down under my feet taking space
between me and a white moon hushed

silent, hushed full, hushed
like the fluttering of my soul
when it is tugged within this space
filled with love in a night-less
time. I dig my heels in this forest
of moonlit dark.

Hush the space. Dance
in my dark soul with light
from a snow-covered forest night.

Lighthouse Tide

The waves of you pull me in to vast emptiness I cherish
The words of ethereal sounds to my heart parishes
On the hill high above the red ants moving sand
Uncovering their tunnels of busy days in the sun
Without your presence and yet I see you in the flash
Of the stranger's eyes with the darkest lashes,
Rosy cheeks are mine when I look away in the second
It took to remember your pull of me into your vapor.
Like the sea mist I walked through when I knew you
Lost in not knowing which way the bird flew
As I tossed out your notes and burned all my letters
Except for the one my heart made to your soul.
The one that rides that wave, the gentle lull
Brings me to you again and again in strange light.

Lion's Lace

Full of grace in her face.
Lines swirled like old vines
imprinted on stone walls
once green and in the light
now torn in certain sections
when life tried to pull away
and dig deep in trenches
lined with bones from past
warriors fighting declawed
and toothless, she peers
through tall grasses,
through me with gold eyes
and I stare back at her wearing
my lace jacket made from a
curtain my mother made out
hand-me-down doilies put out
to protect the fine wood from
forming watermarks from the
tea served in dainty porcelain cups.
Their saucers not enough to
protect the wood from aging and
sold off to the highest bidder.

I bow down to meet her level
of graciousness and pride.
I reach out a hand and touch
the cold nose of a wolf curled
comfortably at my feet,
Unseen and silent she licks my
fingertips, nips at my jacket
until she completely pulls it off
and carries it to the lion as if to
offer my lace as a peace offering.

On Peace, Sestina

I am locked in a little cedar box[1]
tripped me on the floor, opened trap door.
Fell in, head first. Dark well filled my thirst.
Don't tell, lips wrapped around the knot.
The end of the song rings my hot ears
hanging off the side, draining my pride.

I dangled in cedar woods in sight of a lion pride.
Giant paws pawing at what's inside the square box.
Did they hear my learned lessons with pricked ears
Pointy hats kicked down three-mirrored doors
stretched their hands to untwist what is knotted
in chains, behind bars meant to quench a thirst.

These leagues of lessons pour down my thirsty
throat taste sweet over time ripened by pride.
I pull the chains just right to undo the knotted
necklaces, let them swirl neatly in the jewelry box
of cedar alongside the cufflinks and diamond ear-
rings. I see myself a ballerina by the door.

Step out of the heavy lid, hear music like door
chimes, let go of rotten hurts. Like magic by Howard Thurst-
on I float on air with Amelia Ear
heart in the cockpit saying swallow the pride
we're in for a heavenly landing, don't look for the boxed
lines on the ground. They are not

there, wiped clean by the forget-me-nots
covering the lions lying in the morning dew or
the tall grass blades swishing the boxes
of rain drenching our thirsty
empty tongues devoid of lying pride.
She says angels fly with pierced ears,

fills holes in our hearts, in our ears
with gold studs. Flocked gowns knotted
and wrapped around peaceful pride.
Don't be afraid of light from under the door.
There's more self-worth than endless thirst
from being locked in a little cedar box.

I stood on the door step. Rang the pride bell.
Left the unknotted threads in the lock box.
Let my ears bleed what my heart thirsted for – Peace.

Funny Dollar

Pass words let you in,
allow you everything.
Hand it over.
See what's in store.
I know everything
same as you.
I'll take your hand.
Hand in hand
Know everything
Heart keeps beating
I keep breathing.
Talk gossip talk
It was always me.
And I smile back
in secret...ssshhh
Dance, drive, stay alive.
Pass to the left
straighten out to the right
for the long stretch.
You stalk me like the lion I am,
watching, wanting, waiting.
And when we meet it's
penguin feet and daisy meat
under a thousand mirrors.

Morning Stroll

As I pull back on what is pulling me forward, I let go of the leash
and watch myself run free into a neighbor's yard.
Our dogs smile and play bow to each other as
we eat fallen apples from her tree and share stories
of baked goods fresh from the oven on a warm summer morning.

Mystic Ocean Land

I took myself out to the sea, the long yards between breath and
death did not come to me.
I waited for the water to fill my mouth, my throat, and all I felt
was the salt in our tears
drowning out the waves of our arms taking in the space left
between me and you.
We had more years of living out lives we knew we had to do
without our eyes to see
neither me nor you spinning gold circles in the sand making the
chain unbreakable
as breakers crashed down onto rocks scattering the wings of baby
doves still white.
I stood there pointing out the horizon dressed in pink and red
knowing we were not dead
only living another side in between that which is pressed closed
like your lips on my forehead
singing, "'sleep baby baby, slip into the space no one can reach you
until it is safe in the dark."
I closed my eyes and waited on the point; like a pelican
swallowing the fish whole, I was alive.
Published in Adobe Walls 2013

New Mexico Sunset – Greetings from the Swimming Pool

The sky lit up purple this evening like a giant wave of smoke
blowing in from
San Francisco's morning fog coastline.
I grew arms last time I was there bathing in her wine country,
soaking up the purple spilled from shattered glass I broke with
mighty blasts, swinging my arms, taking on the wind wtih my sword.
Fragile pieces pierced my heart, cleared my eyes and I saw it all
so perfectly, the horrors of dinosaurs eating their young desert
fruit too early, tore them off desert paddles, ignoring the fallen.
"What's that slop you got there?" I heard it ask my lover.
I bashed him in the head, let the spines break my skin
in my hands, my shoulders, my back, my heart as I entered
the cool water slowly allowing its body to immerse me.
It was that day I swam for the first time on top of the water,
my chest pulling up above the line with ease I've never felt before.

Pencil

My secret arrogance
creating something from nothing

bring to sharp points
smooth, rounded over,

marked meanings get messy
in the kitchen.

brings pleasures beyond
objects for the bathtub,

leaves fine lead stuck to
finger pads on wallpaper

Chin up, my friend, chin up.

I tap my cheekbones,
stare blankly.
create furiously.
smile happily.
wait wondrously.

Pot of Gold Rain Bubbles

Cold rain cools the heated stench of thoughts gone by.
Bubbles bubble over the rim of the pot full of scum
0r sometimes shiny effervescent colors appear.
I look up to find the rainbow on sunny day through
the sheet of raindrops tapping my shoulders.
The sky was just plain and I thought for a moment….
Perhaps I am where the rainbow ends.
KABOOM a flash of lightning strikes through the blinds.
Oh, what fool am I to think my copper-bottomed pots
hold the keys to my Emerald City as I stir a little salt to taste.
My pot full of greens just a flash in the pan and I swallow
it down whole, gold fillings and all.
Tonight I will wake up astride my horse and give a leg up
to the leprechaun, head for the hills of thunderous lace,
dance in the land of lost pots of golden disgrace blessed
by cherubs who keep them hidden from those who can't smell
their boiled-down essence of weightlessness vanished in the air,
floating in between sun rays and rain drops on a monsoon
summer day.

Star Man

You stand above ten thousand men of ten lifetimes.
Not one could tell me everything your silent thoughts did.
What you knew, the basal, the rhythms, the mystics, poets -
And your lover who stood in the doorway aware of,
how much I didn't know, gave rise to my heart
to meet you above the houses of muffled dreams long after
the tattered letters written in closets scribbled the scramble
of my brain's last panic that I truly had lost you in the dark.

You travel further than the farthest star where I meet you again
standing in timelessness waiting for me in the doorway where
angels convene. Your silk robe untied, open for my skin,
my being to come grow light from my eyes to yours, fit inside
your arms, your legs, your core, your heart. The ballistic wave
that you bounce out reaches me like a palpable soft fairy I've
never felt before, so strong, powerful, beautiful, like you
when I rested my head on your chest hair and felt your mind
incredibly invincible, determined you knew which way to go.

We turned and we twisted fire into gold, melted our teeth,
Fell apart alone in the dark, felt the line on our knees.
You stood up above ten thousand men and rose up, and again
I can hear your command sound off, can hear your legs pound
out lightening strikes to beats of thunder, turn rain into
delicate dew resting in the palm of your hand, and me alongside
whispering sweet dream wishes from the other side of the moon.

Sunrise Fire Death

The fire burns, keeps the pain a constant
wave of solace felt silently by your hand
on your heart. When you whisper quietly
it downs you to the hearth as you poke
the coals and make it roar, jumps out
to catch your hair and you stare back
watch it burning down your house
in little steps along the path to somewhere
higher, higher than all the flames in the pit.
Higher than the highest tip of blue snapping
at you when you wake and see the embers
glowing, never smolder out.
I sing love songs to your heart, still beating
like the drums soldiers march to and
warriors dance with their battle cries heard
in the night by the fire, by your pain.
I say jump, jump above and catch the stars,
one by one, let your feet feel the heat rising
till there's only a cold wind blowing upon
the wings of angels riding doves let free
from the cages, from the pages of tears
landed from fear the fire will never fail.
Hear my voice, and with your eyes closed
take the leap, layer them one upon each
other like stepping stones to where we once
knew each other like newborns on our birthday.
We'll sing a new song with the sun in our eyes.

China Bull – Flash Fiction

The conquistador cried in the night. No tears, just puffy between
the ears about how he conquered via tunnels of red silk, waved
without asking if there'd be valor in the end. Except for the
girl with perfect porcelain skin in the front row, the ring was
practically empty last night in a foreign country.

In the morning, he went downtown for a new show suit. It wasn't
his fault when the saleslady suggested he try it on for size. How it
would fit wasn't the only thing that mattered. A sideways glance
and straight face in her direction caught his mind briefly. During
that moment he knew there was no chance of breaking the bull.

She led him down the narrow hallway. Opened the door, "It will
look good on you."

He maneuvered his muscular legs like a dance on one
foot, cinched the belt tight around the waist, and tore a small hole.
Not noticing, he enjoyed the silky smooth feel on his skin, turning
back around twice before returning the shiny gold sequins to the
tailor.

"Sew them on better," he instructed, "I've no time for sudden
disgrace."

That night the conquistador faltered and fell on his face. When
he looked up he saw her turn bitter. She yelled out at him, "Never
again will I offer you a chance to try it on. You destroyed such
loveliness with your inability to stand straight," and she huffed off
alone in the cold night.

Unnerved at her malevolence, he arranged for the bull to be
slaughtered and brought to her wrapped in billboard posters of

him standing valiant alongside a conquered bull, blood running from where the spears pierced between ribs.

She quickly tore off the paper, burned the meat, and fed it to her Pekingese dog for dinner that night.

For Matt R. Rocks

The cracks are on the side, up the middle, open wide, let the sun shine in, little chicken don't be afraid of love, of flying on magic.

The cracks split open the seed, the rock, the eggshell, my brain from the inside opens up to bloom into eternity, the finite skin holds it together, softly with little slits for my eyes to the light in.

There is no light in the gray of smoky exhaust from idle tailpipes meant to take me to you my love, my one and only pillar in darkness.

The Starfish That Got Away

Five points like my hand
grew wings and flew away.
Flew over the cemetery and hills.
Flew up in the spiral, up and up
Couldn't see any more what was down.
Disappeared like a tiny dot in the sky.
Flew away into the night to shine like a star.
In the moonlight, the fish saw me
just out of reach on a different shore.

R.E. Kooh

Tomorrow hangs up in the doorway with you, side by side
Or with arms around each other as if you were waiting
All the hours and years for me - spun on a dime
Landed flat and neat with the running sound ended,
No echoes, just the ting of metal on a wood dresser.

Unit-Tee's Angel

"It's quite unit-y, I think," she said looking at the Rubik's cube in her hand. "All the little squares within a square. Four sides to fit the box, but where do the wings fit?," the angel asked while waiting in the jury duty waiting room at city hall. She was quite peaceful pondering her puzzle piece which she arranged in solid-colored sides in no time. She decided to put it back exactly the way she found it, all precisely jumbled before putting it down.

She thought perhaps the two women sitting behind her, overhearing their conversation of discord, might get mad at her for even touching it to begin with. It was clear their vice in life was perfection which, of course, neither of them apparently had, not in their spouses or that certain woman they were gossiping about.

The angel said to herself, "Heaven forbade me to get involved with another person's vice. I shan't mess this chance to practice real life once more. This is my millionth time to try it again without being yanked up by my wings. It is hard to keep them under wraps. I hear their vices, see them, feel them and they make me stand guard. This time I am going to simply put this cube down and practice going about life without getting my wings all up and bunched. Dear, dear, now they are criticizing the pair of panties one of them has on. Apparently it's getting all bunched up in her crack….of shit is what I want to say. But I am not going to get involved. No, no." She puts the cube down, rests her hand in her lap and pretends to not hear anything at all.

On Wings - Prose

We all have wings, some of us just don't see them. We are what
came up out of the earth after the dinosaurs left. Like the birds
we grew out of their dirt, their bones, and we have wings in the
ethereal ring of light. Some so delicate and fresh they sit wet and
unattached to our bodies waiting to be hatched free from our
minds. It is in the oldest light of lights where we are released to
seek vision of higher ground on which to see our wings.

Wet flower

naked in the morning sun
Petals glisten reflections of smiling fun
From your lips to mine comes the nectar
Of your kiss pressed into my skin to cure
Midnight's coldness that makes me wither.
Pick me up from this earth. Make me quiver.

Wild Cat at the Card Table

I cheated the cheetah out of his race,
foregoing his long back-legged pace
to tear into the wildebeest at the lake.
There is truth in trying to escape
the hairy turns which make my skin burn.
To making up new names for twisted knots
come pulling up from my throat to soak
up the oil that slicked my birthday candles
the day I thought I could out-race a cheetah.

Fisherman's Prick; Scorpio in Pisces

Another fish caught on a string
Lands on the ledge next to
The scorpion's sting too flat
To reach its eye staring back
Crawls inside the open mouth.
Man's hands reach in the open
Window, runs over the scales
Feels the pinch of the hook.

Black Coffee Guts

It was the coffee that made my stomach turn reflecting my life
upside down.
I ask myself how did I get here and I can see their evil grins
smiling at the sex
With their hands over the cardboard backdrop meant to be the
stage moving
Puppets around, tangling the strings making the marionette dance
and sing
Like they wanted her to because their long arms could reach that
far out
Past the audience, out the door, out in the street to the corner drugstore
Where she would ask for something to make the pain go away and
they'd
Smile their sinister grins again, throw out the candy in open fields
of blue
Oceans and dogs frolicking, saying go get it, watch her bend over
searching.

She Cried

Her tears flowed
into the lake
overflowed
over the damn
bar. She fretted
days and days.
Knocked hard
into the woods.
Killed the hunter.
Wiped clean the laced
Water without a trace

Not Always With Love

Someone asked me if I ever wrote a love poem.
I said if I ever wrote to you it was always a love poem.
Maybe they didn't get how I wrote them; it wasn't
always with love. Sometimes it hit me over the head,
and I wrote how much hurt it caused. Now they know.

Stuck In the House

It was in that stucco house all summer long where I learned how stand on its foundation built to hold up adobe walls and sagging floors. It's where I learned to make stars. I hung them up in the detached garage so I could be closer to them. I learned how to bend myself just right so I wouldn't fall over. I still do, fall over. It's okay though. I tell myself it means I am not really stuck. My feet can slip. My legs can wobble. It means I can dance. I call it the Shakey Dance in the Stucco House. Watch out Fram Liffa, my one legged kick turns into a mean pirouette, so don't get scared. I only want to dance.

Want To See My O-0 Boa Constrictor?

Sure. How big is it?

He is full grown. Last I measured he was 30 ft long before I gave up trying to find his tail.

Take this with you.

Orchids?

Yes, just in case he is hungry. You'll be his friend forever when he knows you can bring him orchid petals. He likes pink ones best.

Cool. How about a pink tutu around his neck while I get a picture of him eating pink orchid petals.

Sure. I don't think he would mind. If you can't bring him orchids, an onion will do.

He likes onions and orchids?

Yes, the O-O boa.

For this one snake, I will wear my own boa made of orchids and onions strung together and I'll fling it across my shoulders as I enter his lair. He'll come wrap around my neck and when he does, will you please take the picture?

Sure, cousin. Anything for you.

Frankenstein's Sacrifice

Holy monster at my door dressed in sin
Two left feet rock and teeter shapeless grin
Faraway howls at the moon blow in the wind
I see him stare with pregnant wife to let him in.
Says there is no room at the Inn, no star to follow
Could he please sleep in the hay filling the hollow
coffin out in my yard. I say cool. Keep the calls low
Looking down at the bumps in her belly giving full blows,
I shut the door to prepare a Halloween baby broth made
special with fresh sprigs of oregano and pumpkin lemonade.

Lou's House on the Right

It is you I skip to with an unconscious beat
In my heart, my head, my being.
When I can longer skip, but trip over dead logs,
It is you I call out to with unconscious words
To save me from the sting of dried wood scraped
On my knees, my palms, and my cheeks.
It is me you find on the bench waiting for my name to be called,
Bent over, sick from all garbage or sitting straight, hands tucked
Under my thighs, smiling at how a bird soars, no movement of wings.
I watch it land next to me and cock its head about in the same silent
Rhythm I heard when I skipped to your house missing all the
cracks.

Train to Buddha Fest

There's a train a coming
Hear it blowing down the wind
Parts it like the red sea
Like a carpet for you and me
Rolling past the stops
jumbled in a jar
Throw it out the window
Throw it down the street
Hear it crumble on the tracks
Never meant to wear cement
in an ocean made of blue
And if you see me coming
with no clothes on my back,
look the other way
There's no room for you to stay
The wind is blowing on the point
Can't you see the train coming
Like a bullet for you and me
It'll fly us to that empty space
we've all been searching for.

The End

If there were answers to all the possibilities,
I wouldn't nibble at my fingernails or
sit and stare at the computer screen or
daydream at all the stoplights about
how it would be to love you
swithout changing a word.